THE COOK-AHEAD COOKBOOK

D0985785

cynthia macgregor

TAYLOR TRADE PUBLISHING

The Cook-Ahead Cookbook, a nitty gritty® Cookbook

©2013 by Taylor Trade Publishing
An imprint of
The Rowman & Littlefield Publishing Group, Inc.
4501 Forbes Boulevard, Suite 200
Lanham, MD 20706
www.rowman.com

Produced by CulinartMedia, Inc.
Design: Harrah Lord
Layout: Patty Holden
Editor: Susan Stover
Photography: Eising Food Photography (all rights reserved)
www.culinartmedia.com

Distributed by National Book Network
1-800-462-6420

ISBN 978-1-58979-887-8
Library of Congress Cataloguing-in-Publication Data on file

Printed in China

CONTENTS

THE BASICS

COMMON PROBLEMS—AND A PLAN

Unexpected changes in your schedule, unexpected guests, or simply low energy are all good reasons to have a fall-back entrée in your freezer. If you avoid takeout, for reasons of economy or taste, and you don't care for commercially prepared frozen entrées, this book offers a relatively easy, home-cooked solution.

The following pages are about cooking main courses and storing them for future meals. It's the main course that normally requires the most thought, time, and preparation. It's the main course upon which most people will judge your dinner, whether it's your guests, your family or yourself.

In this book, you'll find recipes for main dishes featuring poultry (chicken or turkey), beef, veal, pork, sausages, and lamb. There are more recipes for poultry because it's healthy, it's budget-minded, and there are so many things you can do with it.

Not every dinner can be prepared ahead and frozen with the same degree of success, and you won't find recipes for them here. Steaks and roasts are not great candidates for freezing. Neither are foods containing sour cream, yogurt or mayonnaise. Breaded coatings are often soggy when reheated. All the dishes in this cookbook freeze nicely in single-serving packages and can be microwaved or reheated on top of the stove or in the oven with great results.

SIDE DISHES AND VEGETABLES

If your entrée is already prepared, the side dish is easy. A baked potato goes with many meat dishes, and there's nothing easier to fix. Rice is simple and quick, and you can dress up rice quickly and easily by cooking it in chicken broth instead of water and sprinkling in a little thyme and sage, or thyme and rosemary, or freshly cut dill. Or make a simple pasta, or bulgur, barley, beans, or corn.

The vegetable dish is equally easy to deal with. My favorite answer is to whip up a quick salad—lettuce and other raw vegetables, oil and vinegar, herbs and garlic, salt and pepper. You may prefer a more complex creation.

Or serve a fresh steamed vegetable. Even if you prefer fresh vegetables to frozen, keeping a few boxes or bags of frozen vegetables on hand is a good idea.

In some cases, such as in some of the stews, the vegetables and starch are already in the meat and you don't have to prepare anything else at all, though you may want to offer a salad or some garlic bread for a bit of variety.

HERBS

Generally speaking you can substitute fresh herbs, if you have them on hand, for dried herbs called for in these recipes; just triple the amounts. But do not substitute dried dill where fresh dill is called for.

CONTAINERS

There are many commercially produced containers available in which you can successfully freeze your dinners. If you plan to microwave your dinners in the containers, they must be microwavable. Keep several sizes of containers on hand. Plastic freezer bags are good for some dishes. Because I usually transfer the entrée to a sauce-pan to reheat on the stovetop, I find used margarine tubs to be convenient containers.

Do not fill your container completely full, as foods, especially sauces and other liquids, expand when they freeze. Do fill the container almost full-excess air is your enemy—but leave a bit of room for expansion.

For food safety reasons, freeze your creations quickly rather than cooling them on the counter or stove. However, do not take a container full of food freshly hot from the oven or stove and place it so that it is resting on another container in the freezer, or has another container resting on it. If you can't place it on an empty space on the freezer shelf, your next best option is to cool it in the refrigerator and then place it in the freezer.

In the instructions I have included with each recipe, I usually recommend one freezing method for that recipe: "freeze in containers," or "freeze in plastic freezer bags," or "freeze tightly wrapped in aluminum foil." With most of the recipes earmarked for aluminum foil freezing, you really ought to adhere to the suggestion; but in many cases, the question of plastic bags vs. containers is a toss-up.

STORAGE TIME LIMITS

The United States Department of Agriculture recommends keeping cooked meat dishes for a maximum of two to three months and cooked chicken for four to six months (six if it's covered in gravy or sauce). Beyond those times, the flavors and textures will begin to degrade. I have exceeded those limits often, especially when a dish is frozen in a sauce, with good results. There are many variables that affect whether a dish will keep well beyond the recommended time: How many times a day or a week is your freezer door opened? How much air is in the container? Does the dish have a sauce? How well packed is your freezer?

Here are some guidelines:

• Freezers, unlike refrigerators, function best when they're tightly packed.

• Excess air in your storage container will hasten the deterioration of your foods. If storing in a freezer bag, squeeze the air out of the bag before you seal it.

• If a dish has little or no sauce in it consider keeping it less than the recommended time.

REHEATING FROZEN FOODS

It is not necessary to thaw foods before reheating, though you may safely do so (in the refrigerator, not at room temperature) if you wish. If you do thaw foods, decrease the reheating time accordingly. Times given in this book are for defrosting frozen packages of food.

Every recipe will give suggestions for reheating, but here are some basic guidelines:

• 325°F to 350°F is a good oven heat for reheating

• a covered pot on a medium-low burner is a good rule for stovetop reheating

• 70% power is a good setting for microwave reheating

I usually prefer to heat on the stove, rather than the other two options. Obviously, it will take longer to heat enough servings of any recipe to feed four or six people than it will to heat just one for yourself. Also, "medium-low" (or any other setting) on your stove may not produce identical heat to medium-low on another person's stove.

Your cookware makes a difference too—not all saucepans, skillets or Dutch ovens heat at the same rate or evenness. Where I've called for reheating in a covered pot, use a medium saucepan for smaller quantities and a Dutch oven or similar larger pot if you're reheating four or six portions. Do this especially if it's a dish that contains not only meat but vegetables and potatoes too, or a large quantity of sauce.

To reheat on the stovetop, remove food from the container and place in a pot with about ¼ cup water or another liquid in the recipe, such as wine or broth. Cover and cook over medium-low heat for about 25 to 30 minutes or until heated through. Stir and check once or twice during reheating process, adding more water if the liquid level gets too low. If reheating three or more servings, 5 or 10 additional minutes' reheating time may be needed.

To reheat in the microwave, use 50% or 70% microwave power—70% is usually a good choice—and heat for 2 minutes. At the end of 2 minutes, check to see how well heated the food is, and stir so that ingredients are moved from the center of the dish to the edges, if possible. Microwave for another minute or so, depending on the food, number of portions you are reheating and your oven's power. You can restart the microwave as many times as you need to. It is better to err on the side of caution than risk ruining your dinner. Meat and poultry will toughen if overcooked. Stir the food each time you check it. If your container is microwave-safe, you can reheat the food in it. Otherwise, transfer food to a microwave-safe dish.

HOW TO FILL YOUR FREEZER WITH HOME COOKING:

First plan: Prepare any recipe in this book for your evening's dinner, to serve immediately. But cook double what you need. Freeze half the batch to have on hand for that inevitable situation when you'll need to grab something out of the freezer. Do that often enough, with enough different recipes, and the contents of your freezer will soon be the envy of all your friends and neighbors.

Second plan: Set aside a cooking day, or half a day, every so often. Make three recipes; make six; make more. The only boundaries are how much time you have to be in the kitchen, how much food your freezer will hold, and how quickly you think you can use it.

SHORTCUTS

There are only a few recipes in this book that involve a can of soup as an ingredient but there are other shortcuts that I believe in and take full advantage of even when they cost a little more. If you spend time, you save money, but if you spend money, you can save time.

One of these shortcuts is sliced mushrooms—I seldom buy whole ones for a recipe that calls for sliced mushrooms. If my supermarket has fresh sliced mushrooms, I'll pay the premium to save slicing time. If you'd rather save the money, an egg slicer will slice mushrooms quite nicely, and a good deal faster than a knife. For convenience, chopped garlic can be found in bottles in your supermarket but I do not recommend it, as the flavor is not the same. Black olives can be purchased already sliced. Packaged diced ham is sold in most supermarkets. Keep your eye open for other time-saving prepared ingredients.

Another time-saver is meat that's cut to order. If you shop at a customer-friendly supermarket, your butcher can be your best ally. In my supermarket there is no extra charge for cutting meat to the shopper's specifications. If I need chicken cut into 2-inch squares, or cubed beef, or veal chops that are extra-thick, I only need to ask.

Now you have a battle plan. Choose from the following recipes and get ready to do some cooking. You'll never be caught short again. And you'll love the tastiness (and ease!) of the solution.

CHICKEN & TURKEY

LEMON-LIME CHICKEN

SERVES 4

Instead of only lemons, this recipe uses limes as well for a slightly different flavor.

1 chicken, quartered, or leg or breast quarters
Salt, to taste
Freshly ground pepper, to taste
Paprika, to taste
2 Tbsp. vegetable oil
1 cup chicken broth
2 Tbsp. soy sauce
3 cloves garlic, sliced

4 green onions, green and white parts, sliced
¼ cup grated fresh ginger
½ tsp. dried thyme
2 tsp. fresh sage, plus extra for garnish
4 slices fresh lemon
4 slices fresh lime
⅓ cup slivered almonds, optional

Heat oven to 350°F. Season chicken with salt, pepper, and paprika. In a large skillet, heat oil over medium heat. Place chicken in skillet skin-side down and cook until skin is nicely brown.

While chicken is browning, pour broth into a baking pan large enough to hold chicken pieces. Add soy sauce, garlic, green onions, ginger, thyme, and sage. Stir.

When chicken is browned, transfer to baking pan, skin-side up. Tuck a slice of lemon and lime under skin of each piece. Bake for 45 to 50 minutes, or until chicken tests done. If using, add almonds before serving.

Freeze in plastic freezer bags. To reheat on the stovetop or in the microwave, see page 6.

CHICKEN BREASTS WITH TOMATOES & CAPERS

SERVES 4

Capers lend a distinctive flavor to many dishes.

4 boneless, skinless chicken breast halves
Salt, to taste
Freshly ground black pepper, to taste
1 Tbsp. olive oil
1 Tbsp. butter
2 shallots, finely chopped
2 cloves garlic, finely chopped
3 green onions, white and green parts, sliced

1 can (14.5 oz.) diced tomatoes, with juice
2 Tbsp. red wine vinegar
½ cup dry white wine
2 tsp. tomato paste
¼ cup capers with 1 tsp. caper brine
1 tsp. dried tarragon
⅛ cup chopped fresh parsley
¼ cup pine nuts, optional for garnish

Season chicken with salt and pepper. Heat oil and butter over medium heat in a large skillet. Sauté chicken on both sides until lightly browned. Add shallots, garlic, and green onions and cook just until wilted.

Add remaining ingredients, blending thoroughly. Bring to a boil, reduce heat and simmer for 15 minutes, or until chicken tests done. Stir in pine nuts, if using.

Freeze in containers. To reheat on the stovetop or in the microwave, see page 6.

EASY SWEET & HOT CHICKEN

SERVES 4

This chicken dish is so easy you may wind up feeling guilty—with this recipe, almost no work results in a delicious main course. This goes nicely with rice.

1½ cups commercially prepared hot salsa sauce	¼ tsp. dried savory
1 Tbsp. Dijon mustard	1 tsp. lemon juice
1 tsp. ground ginger	4 boneless, skinless chicken breast halves

Heat oven to 350°F. Put all ingredients except chicken in a baking dish big enough to hold all pieces of chicken in one layer. Mix well. Add chicken.

Bake for 30 to 40 minutes or until largest piece of chicken tests done when pierced with a fork.

Freeze in containers or plastic freezer bags. To reheat on the stovetop or in the microwave, see page 6.

LEMON CHICKEN FLORENTINE

SERVES 4

The spinach and fresh ginger in this recipe make it a little different

1 chicken, quartered, or leg or breast quarters
Salt, to taste
Freshly ground pepper, to taste
2 Tbsp. olive oil or other oil
2 cups chicken broth
½ cup dry white wine
2 Tbsp. grated fresh ginger

2 onions, sliced
4 cloves garlic, sliced
1 tsp. dried thyme
1 tsp. dried sage
1 tsp. dried rosemary
4 slices lemon
½ lb. fresh spinach, washed and drained

Heat oven to 350°F. Season chicken with salt and pepper. Heat oil over medium heat in a large skillet. Add chicken to skillet skin-side down and cook until browned.

Pour broth into a large baking pan and add wine, ginger, onions, garlic, thyme, sage, and rosemary. Mix well.

As chicken pieces become browned, place them skin-side up in baking pan. Tuck 1 lemon slice under skin of each chicken piece. When all chicken p/ieces are browned, place baking pan in oven and cook for 35 minutes or until chicken tests done.

Remove pan from oven and tuck spinach around chicken. Return to oven for another 2 minutes.

Freeze in plastic freezer bags. To reheat on the stovetop or in the microwave, see page 6.

BASQUE CHICKEN

SERVES 4

The Basque region straddles the Pyrenees mountain range, bordering southwestern France and northern Spain. It has a distinctive, hearty cuisine with elements of both French and Spanish cooking.

1 chicken, quartered, or leg or breast quarters
2 cloves garlic, minced
Salt, to taste
Freshly ground black pepper, to taste
3 Tbsp. olive oil
½ lb. mushrooms, sliced
1 medium tomato, diced

1 red bell pepper, sliced
1 green bell pepper, sliced
2 medium onions, diced
2 Tbsp. capers with 1 tsp. caper brine
1½ cups stuffed green olives
1 cup pitted black olives
2 bay leaves

Rub chicken with garlic, salt and pepper. Refrigerate, covered, for 1 hour.

Heat oil in a large skillet over medium heat. Brown chicken well on both sides. Remove chicken from pan and set aside. Add mushrooms to pan, sautéing until lightly browned. Return chicken to pan and add all remaining ingredients.

Reduce heat, cover pan and simmer for 30 to 40 minutes, or until chicken tests done. Remove bay leaves.

Freeze in plastic freezer bags. To reheat on the stovetop or in the microwave, see page 6.

FLORIDA CITRUS CHICKEN

SERVES 4

I got this recipe from a friend in Virginia and changed it somewhat. Add honey to counterbalance the tartness of the citrus; add garlic and hot pepper sauce for the added zing. Voila! You've got Florida Citrus Chicken.

1 chicken, quartered, or leg or breast quarters
½ cup lemon juice
½ cup lime juice

½ cup orange juice, or ¼ cup frozen orange juice concentrate
¼ cup honey
3 cloves garlic, quartered
1 Tbsp. Tabasco Sauce

Pierce chicken pieces all over with the tines of a fork. Combine all remaining ingredients in a 1-gallon sealable plastic bag. Add chicken and seal bag tightly. Marinate in the refrigerator for 2 hours.

Heat oven to 350°F. Bake in ½ of the marinade for 30 minutes, or until chicken tests done. Or remove chicken from marinade and grill. If cooked in marinade, remove from marinade before serving.

Freeze in containers or plastic freezer bags. To reheat on the stovetop or in the microwave, see page 6.

CHICKEN WITH MARMALADE

SERVES 4

Here's chicken with a tart-sweet flavor, marrying marmalade, soy sauce, orange juice, and garlic.

4 boneless, skinless chicken breast halves or turkey cutlets
4 cloves garlic, minced
¼ cup soy sauce, divided

1 tsp. dried rosemary
¼ cup orange marmalade, divided
Freshly ground black pepper, to taste
½ cup orange juice

Place chicken pieces in a glass baking dish or casserole. Rub 1 clove of the minced garlic into each piece, leaving garlic on top of chicken after rubbing. Splash 1 table-spoon of the soy sauce on each piece. Sprinkle rosemary on each, and top with 1 tablespoon marmalade. Sprinkle pepper over all and leave covered in the refrigerator for at least 2 hours.

Heat oven to 350°F. Pour orange juice into baking dish and cover. Bake for 20 to 30 minutes or until chicken tests done. Do not turn pieces over while they cook.

Freeze in plastic containers. This reheats best if kept in the same flat position. Reheat in one layer in a covered skillet or in a microwave at 70% power. To reheat on the stovetop or in the microwave, see page 6. Do not overcook or meat will toughen.

CHICKEN ARRABBIATO

SERVES 4

"Arrabbiato" is Italian for angry, and refers to the red pepper in the recipe.

1 pkg. (1 oz.) dried, imported mushrooms
1 chicken, quartered, or leg or breast quarters
Salt, to taste
Freshly ground pepper, to taste
2 cups canned tomatoes, with juice
3 Tbsp. olive oil

12 thin slices hard salami, cut into
    matchstick strips
3 cloves garlic, finely chopped
½ cup dry white wine
1 tsp. red pepper flakes

Reconstitute dried mushrooms for about 1 hour in a bowl with warm water to cover.

Season chicken with salt and pepper. In a saucepan, cook tomatoes until reduced to 1 cup. Heat oil in a large skillet over medium heat. Add chicken to skillet skin-side down, and brown. Turn over to brown second side. While browning, add salami strips, stirring to brown lightly. When browned, remove and set aside.

Pour fat from skillet and add garlic. Cook until wilted but not brown, and add wine. Reduce heat and simmer until reduced by half; add tomatoes.

Squeeze mushrooms to remove excess liquid; reserve ½ cup. Add mushrooms to skillet with reserved liquid. Add red pepper flakes and additional salt and pepper if desired. Return chicken and salami to sauce and cook until chicken tests done.

Freeze in plastic freezer bags. Reheat in a 325°F oven in a baking dish or roasting pan covered tightly with aluminum foil for about 40 minutes.

CHICKEN WITH SALSA & CORN

SERVES 4

This Mexican-style recipe is tasty and particularly easy to prepare.

2 Tbsp. canola oil or other oil
4 boneless, skinless chicken breast halves
1 jar (16 oz.) salsa
1 Tbsp. dark brown sugar
½ tsp. ground coriander

½ tsp. ground cumin
½ tsp. dried oregano
4 thin slices lime
1 can (11–15 oz.) corn kernels

In a large skillet, heat oil over medium heat. Brown chicken very lightly on both sides. Pour off excess oil and reduce heat to medium-low. Add salsa to skillet; add sugar, mixing well. Add coriander, cumin and oregano and mix. Add lime slices to sauce.

Cover and cook for 10 minutes. Add corn and mix into sauce. Cover skillet and cook for 10 minutes, or until chicken tests done.

Freeze in containers. To reheat on the stovetop or in the microwave, see page 6.

TIJUANA CHICKEN

SERVES 4

This bona fide fraud was conceived well north of the border, but is full of hearty Mexican flavors.

1 Tbsp. canola oil
4 boneless, skinless chicken breast halves
Salt, to taste
Freshly ground pepper, to taste
1 large onion, sliced
4 cloves garlic, sliced
1 can (14.5 oz.) diced tomatoes, with juice

1 can (15 oz.) ready-to-eat Cuban-style
    black beans
1 can (11-15 oz.) corn kernels
1 can (4.5 oz.) chopped green chiles, drained
2 Tbsp. lime juice
½ cup chopped green olives
1 jar (6.5 oz.) pimientos, drained and
    coarsely chopped

Heat oil in large skillet over medium heat. Season chicken with salt and pepper. Cook onion and garlic until wilted but not brown. Add chicken and cook for 4 to 6 minutes a side, until lightly browned. Add all remaining ingredients and simmer for 15 minutes, or until chicken is cooked through. Cut into center to test for doneness.

Freeze in containers. To reheat on the stovetop or in the microwave, see page 6.

CHICKEN WITH YOGURT & MUSTARD

SERVES 4

Chicken and mushrooms nestle in a speckled sauce that goes well with noodles, barley or rice. It's an easy recipe to prepare, and it's good for those of you who are watching your weight too.

3 Tbsp. butter
½ lb. mushrooms, sliced
2 containers (8 oz. each) plain yogurt, can be nonfat
2 Tbsp. Dijon mustard

Salt, to taste
Freshly ground pepper, to taste
½ tsp. dried thyme
4 boneless, skinless chicken breast halves or turkey cutlets

Heat oven to 400°F. In a medium or large skillet, heat butter over medium heat. Add mushrooms and sauté until golden.

In a baking dish large enough to hold chicken pieces in one layer, mix yogurt, mustard, salt, pepper, and thyme. Add chicken, turning to coat well. When mushrooms are ready; drain and add to chicken and sauce. Bake for 45 minutes.

Freeze in containers or plastic freezer bags. To reheat on the stovetop or in the microwave, see page 6.

CHICKEN IN DIJON MUSHROOM SAUCE
SERVES 4

This recipe makes a rich, thick, flavorful sauce that goes well with rice or barley. The reconstituted mushrooms augment the mushroom soup that forms the base for the sauce, and the capers give it zing.

1 pkg. (1 oz.) dried imported mushrooms
2 Tbsp. canola oil or other oil
1 Tbsp. butter
1 chicken, quartered, or leg or breast quarters
3 cloves garlic, diced
2 onions, diced
½ lb. button mushrooms, halved
½ cup sherry

2 cans (10.75 oz. each) cream of mushroom soup, undiluted
1 Tbsp. plus 1 tsp. Dijon mustard
2 tsp. Worcestershire sauce
2 tsp. paprika
1 Tbsp. fresh rosemary
2 tsp. capers, drained

Reconstitute mushrooms for 1 hour in a bowl with enough warm water to cover.

Heat oil and butter in a large skillet over medium heat. Add chicken, garlic, and onions, and cook until chicken is lightly browned on both sides. Squeeze excess water out of reconstituted mushrooms and add to skillet.

Reduce heat to medium-low and add remaining ingredients. Cover and cook for 20 to 30 minutes more, or until chicken tests done. Turn once during cooking.

Freeze in containers or in plastic freezer bags. To reheat on the stovetop or in the microwave, see page 6.

CHICKEN CURRY

SERVES 4

Adjust the amount of curry powder to your taste. If you buy chicken precut, it will save some time. This curry is good with rice and broccoli.

2 containers (8 oz. each) plain yogurt	Flour to coat chicken
1 Tbsp. curry powder, or to taste	2 Tbsp. vegetable oil
2 Tbsp. chopped fresh basil	1 red onion, cut into strips
1 chicken, quartered, or leg or breast quarters	1 green bell pepper, cut into strips
	1 red bell pepper, cut into strips

Mix yogurt, curry powder and basil together in a bowl. Cover and refrigerate for a few minutes to blend flavors.

Toss chicken pieces in enough flour to coat. Heat oil in a large skillet or wok over high heat. When it begins to smoke, add chicken in small batches to brown on all sides. As they brown, remove and set aside. Add onion and peppers to pan. Stir until wilted and onion begins to turn golden.

Return chicken to pan and add yogurt mixture. Reduce heat to medium-low, stir contents of pan well and cook for about 30 minutes. When chicken is cooked through and sauce has thickened, the dish is done. Freeze in containers or plastic freezer bags. To reheat on the stovetop or in the microwave, see page 6.

CHICKEN BREASTS WITH MUSTARD SAUCE

SERVES 4

The mustard sauce makes this a rich and delicious main course.

1 Tbsp. butter

4 boneless, skinless chicken breast halves

Salt, to taste

Freshly ground pepper, to taste

1 small onion, minced

¼ tsp. dried thyme

1 Tbsp. red wine vinegar

¼ cup dry white wine

½ cup chicken broth

2 tsp. tomato paste

¼ cup heavy cream

1 Tbsp. Dijon mustard

Heat butter in a large skillet over medium heat. Sprinkle chicken breasts with salt and pepper. Add breasts to skillet and cook on each side until starting to brown. Remove and set aside.

Add onion and thyme to skillet, cooking just until onion is wilted. Add vinegar and wine and bring to a medium boil. Add broth and tomato paste, stirring tomato paste well into mixture, and cook at a medium boil for about 7 minutes.

While sauce cooks, cut chicken into bite-size pieces. After 7 minutes, add cream and mustard, stirring with each addition. Reduce heat, return chicken to skillet and coat with sauce. Simmer for 3 minutes.

Freeze in containers. To reheat on the stovetop or in the microwave, see page 6.

EAST MEETS WEST CHICKEN

SERVES 4

If you store ginger in a covered jar in white vermouth or vodka, it will keep forever, and you will always have "fresh" ginger available for cooking.

2 Tbsp. peanut oil or other oil
¼ cup grated fresh ginger
4 green onions, white and green parts, thinly sliced
4 cloves garlic, thinly sliced
4 boneless, skinless chicken breast halves, cut into strips
Juice of ½ lime
¼ cup soy sauce

1 cup chicken broth
½ tsp. nutmeg
I red bell pepper, sliced
2 carrots, peeled and sliced into coins
½ lb. shiitake or button mushrooms
½ lb. snow peas
1 can (8 oz.) Chinese baby corn, drained
1 can (7 oz.) sliced water chestnuts

Heat oil in a large skillet over medium heat. Add ginger, green onions, and garlic. Stir until slightly wilted. Add chicken strips, and sauté until lightly browned.

When chicken is browned, combine lime juice, soy sauce, chicken broth, and nutmeg, and pour broth mixture over chicken and reduce heat to medium-low. Cover skillet and cook for about 10 minutes, turning once. Add bell pepper, carrots, mushrooms, peas, corn, and water chestnuts about 5 minutes before end of cooking time.

Freeze in plastic freezer bags. To reheat on the stovetop or in the microwave, see page 6.

PEANUT CHICKEN

SERVES 3

The flavors of Thai chicken saté are so delicious; I wanted to create something similar in a recipe that would freeze successfully. This is the result.

3 Tbsp. smooth peanut butter, prefer additive-free
3 Tbsp. plum jam or chutney
2 Tbsp. water
½ tsp. lemon juice
1½ tsp. soy sauce
1 tsp. sesame oil

2 tsp. olive oil
½ tsp. ground ginger
3 boneless, skinless chicken breast halves, cut into bite-size pieces
¼ cup sliced green onion, white part only

Prepare peanut sauce: In a small bowl, blend peanut butter, jam or chutney, water, lemon juice, soy sauce, and sesame oil with the back of a spoon until well blended and smooth.

Heat olive oil in a large skillet over medium-high heat. Add ginger to oil and mix well. Add chicken and brown quickly, stirring, until pieces are cooked through. With a slotted spoon, remove chicken and set aside. Drain oil from pan.

Return chicken to pan immediately, add peanut sauce and stir to coat. Mix in green onion.

Freeze in containers. Reheat food in its container, in the microwave at 50% power. Length of time will depend on your microwave and on how many portions or containers you heat at one time: start with 4 minutes per portion and test often. See page 6.

CHICKEN ABLAZE
SERVES 4

So named for its peppery punch. You are free to adjust the heat to suit your taste.

2 Tbsp. canola oil or other oil
1 chicken, quartered, or leg or breast quarters
1 cup chopped celery
2 cups chopped onion
1 green bell pepper, diced

2 cups tomato juice
6 Tbsp. cider vinegar
Salt, to taste
Freshly ground pepper to taste
¾ tsp. Tabasco Sauce, or to taste

Heat oven to 350°F. In a large skillet, heat oil over medium heat. When oil is hot, add chicken and cook until browned. Remove and place in a baking dish large enough to hold pieces in one layer.

Add celery, onion and bell pepper to skillet and cook until wilted. Add remaining ingredients to skillet and bring to a boil. Simmer for 2 minutes and pour over chicken in baking dish. Bake uncovered for 40 to 50 minutes, until thoroughly cooked, basting 2 or 3 times during cooking.

Freeze in plastic freezer bags. Reheat in a 325°F oven in a baking dish or small roasting pan covered tightly with aluminum foil for about 35 minutes.

CHICKEN WITH ARTICHOKES

SERVES 4

This is another chicken dish that's elegant enough for guests.

3 Tbsp. olive oil
4 boneless, skinless chicken breast halves,
    cut into 2-inch-square pieces
2 cloves garlic, finely chopped
½ lb. mushrooms, sliced
4 thin lemon slices
1 Tbsp. flour
Salt, to taste

Freshly ground pepper, to taste
½ tsp. dried oregano
¼ tsp. dried thyme
¼ tsp. dried savory
½ cup dry white wine
1 can (14 oz.) unmarinated artichoke hearts,
    drained and quartered

Heat oil in a large skillet over medium heat until hot. Add chicken and cook, turning, until opaque on all sides. Remove and set aside.

Add garlic, mushrooms, and lemon slices to skillet. Cook until mushrooms are tender and have changed color. Sprinkle flour and seasonings into skillet and cook for 1 minute, stirring.

Add wine and bring to a boil stirring. When mixture thickens, add artichoke hearts and chicken. Reduce heat and simmer until chicken tests done.

Freeze in containers. To reheat on the stovetop or in the microwave, see page 6.

BASIL CHICKEN

SERVES 4

This is very good with fresh basil, but either fresh or dried will work.

4 boneless, skinless chicken breast halves,
    cut into bite-size pieces
Salt, to taste
Freshly ground pepper, to taste
Paprika, to taste
2 Tbsp. canola oil or olive oil

1 clove garlic, sliced
½ cup chicken broth
½ cup dry white wine
1 Tbsp. chopped fresh basil or 1 tsp. dried
1 tomato, diced
½ cup heavy cream

Season chicken with salt, pepper, and paprika. Heat oil in a large skillet over medium heat. Add chicken and cook for 5 minutes on each side. Two minutes after turning, add garlic slices.

When chicken has been cooked on both sides, add broth and wine. Bring to a boil, reduce heat, cover and simmer for 5 minutes. Add basil, tomato and cream. Simmer for 5 minutes, or until chicken tests done.

Freeze in containers. To reheat on the stovetop or in the microwave, see page 6.

BRUNSWICK STEW

SERVES 4 TO 6

I've seen many recipes for Brunswick stew most calling for chicken as the main ingredient but a few calling for meats as exotic as squirrel! In this version the ingredients are all familiar.

2 Tbsp. vegetable oil
2 medium onions, thinly sliced
2 cloves garlic, finely chopped
4 turkey cutlets or boneless, skinless chicken
    breast halves, sliced thinly
1 jar pimientos, small or large jar
1 red bell pepper, cut into bite-size pieces
Salt, to taste
Freshly ground pepper, to taste

1 Tbsp. plus 1 tsp. brown sugar
½ small lemon, thinly sliced
¾ cup dry sherry
2 bay leaves
6 drops Tabasco Sauce
¼ tsp. dried turmeric
1 cup water or chicken or vegetable broth
1 cup frozen lima beans, optional

In a medium skillet, heat oil. Add onions and garlic and cook until translucent. Place onions, garlic and all remaining ingredients in a pot large enough to hold them and cook over medium-low heat for about 30 minutes, until turkey is properly cooked and flavors are blended. Remove bay leaves.

Freeze in plastic freezer bags or larger containers. To reheat on the stovetop or in the microwave, see page 6.

CHICKEN KORMA

SERVES 4

Korma is a spicy curry dish from India or Pakistan. Here's a variation for chicken that's easy to cook. The results are delicious. Serve it with rice and a vegetable of your choice.

2 cups plain yogurt
2 ½ Tbsp. curry powder, or to taste
2 tsp. salt
2 tsp. ground coriander
2 tsp. minced fresh ginger
8 cloves garlic, minced
1 tsp. cayenne or red pepper flakes, or to taste

1 tsp. lemon juice
4 boneless, skinless chicken breast halves
1 Tbsp. canola oil
1 medium onion, chopped
1 large tomato, peeled and chopped
2 bay leaves

In a large bowl, combine yogurt, curry powder, salt, coriander, ginger, garlic, cayenne, and lemon juice. Stir well, add chicken and stir again to coat well. Cover bowl and marinate in the refrigerator for at least 1 hour; longer is better.

Heat oil in a large skillet over medium heat. Add onion and cook until lightly browned. Stir in tomato and bay leaves and cook for 5 minutes. Add chicken and marinade and mix well. Reduce heat, cover and simmer for about 30 minutes, stirring occasionally. Remove bay leaves.

Freeze in containers. To reheat on the stovetop or in the microwave, see page 6. On the stovetop, use a skillet and check frequently to avoid burning or drying sauce.

BAKED CHICKEN IN BARBECUE SAUCE

SERVES 4

The flavors of grilled chicken are possible even without the grill when you cook it in this barbecue sauce.

4 boneless, skinless chicken breast halves
½ cup ketchup
½ cup vegetable oil
½ cup cider vinegar
2 Tbsp. Worcestershire sauce
4 drops Tabasco Sauce
½ cup brown sugar, packed
2 heaping tsp. Dijon mustard
1 tsp. ground ginger
2 cloves garlic, pressed
Juice of 1 medium lemon
Salt, to taste
Freshly ground pepper, to taste

Heat oven to 350°F. Place chicken breast halves in a baking dish large enough to hold all pieces in single layer.

In a saucepan, combine all remaining ingredients and stir well. Bring to a boil, pour over chicken and bake for about 30 minutes, or until thickest part of largest piece of chicken tests done.

Freeze in containers or plastic freezer bags. Reheat in a 325°F oven in a baking pan or roasting pan covered tightly with aluminum foil for about 35 minutes. Or reheat on the stovetop or in the microwave; see page 6.

CHICKEN PAPRIKA

SERVES 4

Paprika combines with lemon, garlic, rosemary, and cayenne pepper to give this chicken dish oomph.

3 Tbsp. olive oil
5 cloves garlic, minced
Juice and zest of 1 lemon
4 boneless, skinless chicken breast halves
Salt, to taste
Freshly ground black pepper, to taste

1 Tbsp. plus 1 tsp. chopped fresh rosemary
1 tsp. dried thyme
¼ cup paprika
Cayenne pepper, to taste
2 cups chicken broth

Heat oven to 350°F. Heat oil in a medium skillet over medium heat. Sauté garlic until wilted. Add lemon juice and zest and cook for 2 minutes.

Season chicken with salt and pepper and place in a baking dish large enough to hold all pieces of chicken in single layer. Sprinkle with rosemary, thyme, paprika and cayenne. Pour oil-garlic-lemon mixture over chicken and add chicken broth. Cover with aluminum foil and bake for 15 minutes. Uncover and bake for 15 minutes.

Freeze in containers. Reheat in a 350°F oven in a baking dish in single layer. Cover tightly with aluminum foil and heat for about 40 minutes.

HONEY GARLIC CHICKEN

SERVES 4

A little sweet and a little sharp, this recipe offers the yin and yang —honey and garlic—of sauce for chicken.

2 Tbsp. olive oil or other oil
4 boneless, skinless chicken breast halves
½ cup chicken broth
¼ cup honey

¼ cup soy sauce
2 Tbsp. ketchup
3 cloves garlic, minced

Heat oil in a large skillet over medium heat. Add chicken and cook until lightly browned on both sides.

Heat broth in a saucepan over medium heat. When broth simmers, turn off heat and add remaining ingredients, stirring vigorously and blending well.

Drain any fat from skillet and pour sauce over chicken in skillet. Reduce heat, cover and simmer for about 25 minutes.

Freeze in containers or plastic freezer bags. To reheat on the stovetop or in the microwave, see page 6.

EASY POULTRY À LA KING

SERVES 4 TO 6

This is a great recipe for leftover holiday turkey or cooked chicken. Expand or reduce the recipe according to the amount of cooked poultry available.

2 Tbsp. butter or margarine

1 lb. mushrooms, sliced

2 cans (10.75 oz. each) cream of mushroom
   soup, undiluted

1 cup sherry

1 medium onion, minced

1 red bell pepper, diced

1 carrot, thinly sliced

1 tsp. dried sage

1 tsp. dried thyme

Salt, to taste

Freshly ground pepper, to taste

4–6 cups diced cooked turkey or chicken

¼ cup chopped fresh dill

Melt butter in a large skillet over medium heat and sauté mushrooms until lightly golden. In a large saucepan, heat soup and sherry over medium-low heat stirring to blend and remove any lumps.

Add vegetables and seasonings to soup mixture. Reduce heat, stir and simmer for 10 or 15 minutes. Add turkey and dill and cook for 10 minutes.

Freeze in containers or plastic freezer bags. To reheat on the stovetop or in the microwave, see page 6. Use water or sherry. If adding sherry during cooking, be sure to continue simmering for a few minutes.

TURKEY IN ROSEMARY ORANGE SAUCE

SERVES 4

Orange juice adds a nice flavor to poultry. Try this and you'll become slightly addicted, as I am.

4 turkey cutlets or 4 boneless, skinless
    chicken breast halves
Salt, to taste
Freshly ground black pepper, to taste
3 Tbsp. vegetable oil, divided
¼ cup finely chopped shallots

3 cloves garlic, minced
¾ cup orange juice
½ cup chicken broth
1 tsp. butter
1 tsp. chopped fresh rosemary
½ tsp. wine vinegar

Season both sides of turkey with salt and pepper. In a large skillet over medium high heat, heat ½ of the oil. Add turkey and sear until well browned on both sides. Remove and set aside.

Reduce heat to medium and add remaining oil. When hot, add shallots and garlic. Cook, stirring, for about 1 minute. Add orange juice and broth. Bring to a simmer and cook until reduced by half, about 3 minutes.

Return turkey to pan, along with any juices that have accumulated. Reduce heat to a simmer and cook until turkey is done. Add butter, rosemary, and vinegar to pan and stir well into sauce. Add additional salt and freshly ground pepper to taste, if needed.

Freeze in containers. To reheat on the stovetop or in the microwave, see page 6.

BAKED TURKEY FESTA

SERVES 4 TO 5

Turkey and Italian sausage make a happy couple—and the "wedding" is right in your kitchen! You can use mild or hot sausage, according to your taste—I prefer the hot variety.

1 Tbsp. olive oil or other oil

1 lb. Italian sausage, mild or hot, cut into chunks

3 lb. turkey breast, cut into 4 or 5 serving pieces, or 1 chicken, cut into serving pieces

2 onions, chopped

4 cloves garlic, chopped

1 green bell pepper, diced

1 cup frozen peas

2 cans (15 oz. each) tomato sauce

½ cup red wine

3 Tbsp. tomato paste

1 Tbsp. Worcestershire sauce

3 drops Tabasco Sauce

1 bay leaf

1 tsp. dried basil

1 tsp. dried oregano

Heat oven to 350°F. In a large skillet over medium heat, heat oil. Add sausage and turkey and cook until browned.

Add all remaining ingredients to a baking pan large enough to hold turkey and sausage pieces in a single layer. Mix well. As turkey and sausage pieces become browned, transfer them to baking pan. When all pieces are browned, bake for 40 minutes, or until turkey tests done. Remove bay leaf.

Freeze in plastic freezer bags. To reheat on the stovetop or in the microwave, see page 6.

TURKEY ABBONDANZA

SERVES 4

"Abbondanza" is Italian for plenty. The green okra, peppers, and celery contrast with the rich red sauce to make this attractive as well as tasty.

2 Tbsp. olive oil

4 turkey cutlets or 1 chicken, quartered, or favorite pieces (leg or breast quarters)

2 cups prepared marinara sauce

½ cup red wine

1 green bell pepper, diced

1 lb. okra, ends removed, sliced

1 cup thinly sliced celery

2 onions, chopped

½ tsp. dried basil

½ tsp. dried oregano

½ lb. mushrooms, sliced

Heat oven to 350°F. Heat oil in a large skillet over medium heat. Place turkey or chicken in skillet and cook, turning, until browned.

Mix all remaining ingredients except mushrooms in a baking pan large enough to hold turkey pieces in single layer. When turkey is browned, remove from skillet and place pieces in baking pan. Add mushrooms to skillet and sauté until lightly golden. Remove mushrooms and distribute evenly in baking pan. Bake for 40 minutes, or until turkey tests done.

Freeze in plastic freezer bags. To reheat on the stovetop or in the microwave, see page 6.

MICHIGAN POULTRY STEW

SERVES 6

This Midwestern dish is hearty, slightly sweet and bound to please your family, your guests and yourself.

2 Tbsp. butter
2 medium leeks, sliced into rings
4 cloves garlic, coarsely chopped
12 baby carrots, peeled and left whole, if small
4 large potatoes, peeled and cut into eighths
1 tsp. dried savory
¼ tsp. dried marjoram

2 lb. boneless, skinless chicken breast halves
    or turkey cutlets, cut into smaller pieces
2 tsp. red wine vinegar
1 tsp. brown sugar
4 cups chicken broth
½ cup dry white wine
2 pinches cayenne pepper
Salt, to taste

In a Dutch oven or similar pot, melt butter over low heat. Add leeks and garlic, cover and cook for 10 minutes. Remove lid and add carrots and potatoes. Stir, cover and cook for 15 minutes.

Add all remaining ingredients and cover. Raise heat to medium-low and cook for another 30 minutes, or until potatoes are done. Stir occasionally while cooking.

Freeze in plastic freezer bags. To reheat on the stovetop or in the microwave, see page 6.

CHILI CHICKEN
SERVES 4

If you love the flavor of chili; if you prefer chicken to beef; if you're tired of the same old chili; or if you're just looking for a new twist on chicken —this recipe is right up your alley.

2 Tbsp. canola oil or other oil
2 onions, chopped
1 can (14.5 oz.) diced tomatoes, with juice
6 tsp. chili powder, divided
1 tsp. dried oregano

½ tsp. ground cumin
4 boneless, skinless chicken breast halves
    or turkey cutlets
Salt, to taste

Heat oven to 350°F. Heat oil in a medium skillet over medium heat and cook onions until translucent. Transfer to a baking dish large enough to hold chicken pieces in single layer. Add tomatoes, 4 teaspoons of the chili powder, oregano, and cumin. Mix well.

Sprinkle chicken with salt and remaining 2 teaspoons chili powder, and rub into chicken. Place chicken pieces on top of tomato mixture. Bake uncovered for about 30 minutes, or until chicken tests done.

Freeze in containers or plastic freezer bags. Reheat in a 350°F oven in a baking dish covered tightly with aluminum foil for about 35 minutes, or reheat on the stovetop or in the microwave; see page 6.

PORK, SAUSAGE & LAMB

PORK MEATBALLS IN CRANBERRY-TOMATO SAUCE

SERVES 6 TO 8

This flavorful meatball dish is a delicious alternative to ordinary beef meatballs.

2 jars (16 oz. each) medium or hot salsa
2 cans (16 oz. each) jellied cranberry sauce
3 lb. ground pork
½ cup breadcrumbs
2 medium onions, finely diced
3 cloves garlic, pressed
Salt, to taste

Freshly ground pepper, to taste
½ tsp. dried sage
¼ tsp. nutmeg
⅛ cup chopped fresh dill
1 egg, beaten
3 Tbsp. vegetable oil

Over medium heat combine salsa and cranberry sauce in a Dutch oven or similar large pot. While sauce heats, mix together pork, breadcrumbs, onions, garlic, salt pepper, sage, nutmeg, dill, and egg, and blend well.

Heat oil over medium heat in large skillet. Form meat mixture into meatballs and brown meatballs on all sides, transferring to Dutch oven when browned. Cook over medium-low heat for 30 minutes.

Freeze in containers or in plastic freezer bags. To reheat on the stovetop or in the microwave, see page 6.

MAPLE PORK TENDERLOIN

SERVES 3

The sweet flavors of orange juice and maple syrup complement this lean cut of pork.

1 pork tenderloin, about ¾ lb.
1 medium onion, diced
¼ cup orange juice, divided
¼ cup maple syrup, divided
2 Tbsp. dry white wine

2 Tbsp. soy sauce
Freshly ground pepper, to taste
2 cloves garlic, minced
1 Tbsp. olive oil
½ cup chicken broth

Trim any fat from pork. Make a marinade by combining onion, 2 tablespoons orange juice, 2 tablespoons maple syrup, wine, soy sauce, pepper, and garlic. Mix in a bowl or freezer bag, add tenderloin and cover or seal. Marinate in the refrigerator for at least 2 hours.

Heat oven to 400°F. In a medium skillet, heat oil over medium heat. Remove pork from marinade and place in skillet, reserving marinade. Cook for 5 minutes, turning to brown evenly. Transfer pork to a small baking pan and bake for 30 minutes.

About 20 minutes into baking process, pour reserved marinade into a saucepan and add remaining orange juice, remaining maple syrup, and broth. Over medium high heat, bring to a boil, reduce heat and simmer for about 5 minutes, or until sauce thickens slightly. Use as gravy for pork.

Slice into ¼-inch rounds and freeze each serving (⅓ of the slices with ⅓ of the sauce) in a plastic freezer bag. To reheat on the stovetop or in the microwave, see page 6.

PORK CHOP CASSEROLE

SERVES 6

Here's another all-in-one meal, offering rice, green peppers, and pork chops in a tomato-based sauce. Serve this with French bread or garlic bread, with a nice salad or even with an additional vegetable.

1 can (15 oz.) tomato sauce
1 cup red wine
1 tsp. Worcestershire sauce
¼ tsp. dried marjoram
½ tsp. dried savory

½ tsp. cayenne pepper
6 pork chops, ½-inch thick
1 onion, chopped
2 green bell peppers, diced
2 cups uncooked rice

Heat oven to 350°F. Use a baking dish or roasting pan large enough to hold 6 chops in single layer. Pour tomato sauce into baking dish; add wine, Worcestershire, herbs, and cayenne, and mix. Place chops in baking dish. Add onion, bell peppers, and rice in sauce around chops.

Cover baking dish with foil and bake for 45 minutes.

Freeze each portion in a plastic freezer bag or in a container. Reheat in a 350°F oven in a baking dish or roasting pan covered tightly with aluminum foil for about 35 minutes.

MEDITERRANEAN PORK CHOPS

SERVES 4

Your dish will taste even more Mediterranean if your herbs are fresh. If you have fresh herbs on hand, use triple the dried quantity.

4 lean, thick, preferably center-cut, pork chops
Salt, to taste
Freshly ground pepper, to taste
2 Tbsp. olive oil
2 medium onions, finely chopped
4 cloves garlic, minced
1 red bell pepper, cut into bite-size strips
1 yellow bell pepper, cut into bite-size strips
1 green bell pepper, cut into bite-size strips

1 cup chicken broth
2 Tbsp. red wine vinegar
1 can (15 oz.) crushed tomatoes, with juice
1 tsp. ground cumin
1 bay leaf
½ tsp. dried rosemary
1 tsp. dried thyme
1 tsp. dried basil
½ cup sliced, pitted black olives

Season chops with salt and pepper on both sides. Heat oil over medium-high heat in a skillet large enough to hold all 4 chops at once. Brown chops well on each side. Pour off almost all fat, retaining about 1 tablespoon and reduce heat to medium-low.

Add onions and garlic, and cook until wilted. Add peppers. Cook for 1 minute. Add broth, vinegar, tomatoes, cumin, herbs, and additional salt if desired. Reduce heat to low, cover and cook for 20 minutes. Remove from heat, remove bay leaf. Add olives.

Freeze in plastic freezer bags or in containers. Heat in a 350°F oven in a baking dish or roasting pan tightly covered with aluminum foil for 25 to 40 minutes.

TURKISH-STYLE MEATBALLS

SERVES 4

For meatballs with a difference, use lamb and rice instead of beef and breadcrumbs. These Turkish-style meatballs have a little sauce, and they're moist and flavorful. They taste good in pita bread with a little minted yogurt and fresh tomatoes.

1 lb. lean ground lamb
1 medium onion, finely chopped
¼ cup uncooked rice
2 Tbsp. fresh parsley, minced
Salt, to taste

Freshly ground pepper, to taste
2 eggs, beaten
1 cup olive oil or other oil
1 jar (16 oz.) tomato sauce

Mix together meat, onion, rice, parsley, salt, pepper, and eggs. Knead until well mixed. Form into meatballs about 1 inch in diameter. Recipe should make about 16 meatballs.

Heat oil over medium-high heat in a skillet large enough to hold all meatballs. When surface of oil shimmers, carefully place meatballs in hot oil. Fry for 5 minutes, turning as needed to brown all sides. Drain oil from skillet. Heat tomato sauce in skillet and add meatballs. Heat for 10 minutes.

Freeze each serving wrapped in aluminum foil. Reheat in a 350°F oven in aluminum foil on a baking sheet for about 25 minutes.

GRANNY SMITH PORK STEW

SERVES 6 TO 8

Granny Smith apples and pearl onions combine in a special pork dish.

3 cups apple juice
1 cup beef broth
½ tsp. ground ginger
¼ tsp. dried basil
½ tsp. dried sage
¼ tsp. mace
⅛ tsp. ground cloves

½ tsp. cayenne pepper
1 cup sherry
3 Tbsp. vegetable oil
3 lb. pork tenderloin, cut into 2-inch slices
1 pkg. (16 oz.) frozen pearl onions or small onions
1 Granny Smith apple or other tart variety

Heat apple juice over medium-low heat in a Dutch oven or similar large pot and add beef broth. Add ginger, basil, sage, mace, cloves, cayenne, and sherry. Simmer uncovered.

Heat oil in a large skillet over medium heat. Add pork and cook until lightly browned. When pork is browned, transfer to Dutch oven. When all pork is in Dutch oven, adjust heat so sauce is simmering, cover and cook for 45 minutes. Near the end of the cooking time, add onions and cook for 10 minutes.

Peel and core apple and cut into quarters. Cut each quarter into 4 pieces. Add apple to stew and cook for 4 minutes.

Freeze in plastic freezer bags. To reheat on the stovetop or in the microwave, see page 6.

CARAWAY PORK CHOPS

SERVES 4

Wine and caraway seeds add a distinctive flavor to these chops. Use other fresh herbs besides the dill if you have them on hand—remember, use triple the amount of dried.

2 Tbsp. peanut oil or other oil
½ lb. mushrooms, sliced
2 tsp. paprika
2 tsp. garlic powder
½ tsp. dried rosemary
½ tsp. dried sage

½ tsp. dried thyme
4 boneless pork chops, ½-inch thick
1 large onion, diced
1 cup dry white wine
2 tsp. caraway seeds
¼ cup chopped fresh dill

Heat oil in a large skillet over medium-high heat. Add mushrooms, sautéing until lightly golden. Mix together paprika, garlic powder, rosemary, sage, and thyme, and rub mixture into both sides of chops.

Remove mushrooms from skillet and set aside. Reduce heat to medium. Add chops and onion to skillet and brown chops on both sides. Add wine and return mushrooms to pan. Reduce heat until wine just simmers and add caraway seeds. Simmer for 30 to 40 minutes, or until chops are tender. Remove from heat, add dill and stir to mix.

Freeze each chop with sauce in a plastic freezer bag or container. Reheat in a 350°F oven in a baking dish or roasting pan tightly covered with aluminum foil for about 35 minutes.

PORK & SWEET POTATO STEW

SERVES 4

For faster prep, have your supermarket cube the meat for you.

3 Tbsp. butter or margarine

½ lb. mushrooms

2 large onions, chopped

3 cloves garlic, chopped

1 Tbsp. olive oil

3 lb. lean pork, trimmed of fat, cut into
   2-inch cubes

2 cans (14.5 oz. each) diced tomatoes
   including juice

1 cup chicken broth

½ cup dry white wine

2 bay leaves

1½ tsp. dried sage

Salt, to taste

Freshly ground pepper, to taste

2 large sweet potatoes, peeled and cut
   into bite-size pieces

1 can (11 oz.) corn kernels

Over medium-high heat in a large skillet melt butter and sauté mushrooms. When not yet fully browned, add onions and cook until translucent. Transfer mushrooms and onions to a Dutch oven. Add garlic to skillet and cook until just beginning to brown. Remove and add to Dutch oven.

Heat oil in skillet. Brown pork on all sides, removing to Dutch oven as cubes brown. Add tomatoes, broth, wine, bay leaves, sage, salt, and pepper. Bring to a boil, reduce heat, cover and simmer for 30 minutes. Add sweet potatoes and corn and cook, covered, for 1 hour, or until pork is tender. Remove bay leaves.

Freeze in individual servings in plastic freezer bags. To reheat on the stovetop or in the microwave, see page 6.

RED VELVET PORK STEW

SERVES 4 TO 6

2 Tbsp. vegetable oil
2 lb. lean pork, cut into 2-inch cubes
4 cloves garlic, sliced
2 medium onions, sliced
2 stalks celery, sliced
3 Tbsp. butter
1 lb. mushrooms, sliced
1 can (15 oz.) crushed tomatoes, with juice
2 cans (15 oz. each) tomato sauce

1 green bell pepper, cut into bite-size strips
1 cup red wine
1 Tbsp. Worcestershire sauce
1 Tbsp. chopped fresh cilantro
½ tsp. dried turmeric
1 tsp. dried basil
1 tsp. dried oregano
Freshly ground pepper, to taste
2 small carrots or 1 large, cut into ¼-inch slices

Heat oil in a large skillet over medium-high heat. Brown pork cubes on all sides, transferring to a Dutch oven or similar large pot when browned. Sauté garlic and onions until beginning to brown, transferring to large pot as they finish. Sauté celery for 2 minutes and add to pot.

Heat butter in skillet and sauté mushrooms; add to large pot. Add all remaining ingredients, bring to a boil, reduce heat, cover and simmer for 1½ hours. When pork is tender, add carrots and cook for 10 minutes.

Freeze in plastic freezer bags. To reheat on the stovetop or in the microwave, see page 6.

GOLDEN PORK CHOPS

SERVES 4

Peaches complement the pork beautifully in this slightly unusual dish.

2 Tbsp. vegetable oil
4 medium pork chops, with bones
1 can (8 oz.) tomato sauce
¼ cup brown sugar, packed
½ tsp. cinnamon
¼ tsp. ground cloves

¼ cup vinegar
1 can (29 oz.) cling peach halves, drained,
    ¼ cup syrup reserved
Salt, to taste
Freshly ground pepper, to taste

In a large skillet, heat oil over medium heat. Lightly brown pork chops on both sides, pouring off excess fat when browned. While chops are browning, mix tomato sauce, sugar, cinnamon, cloves, vinegar and reserved peach syrup.

Heat oven to 350°F. Place browned chops in a baking dish large enough to hold them in a single layer. Pour tomato sauce-syrup mixture over chops and add salt and pepper. Top with peach halves. Cover baking dish with aluminum foil and bake for 25 to 45 minutes, depending on thickness of chops, or until chops are thoroughly cooked.

Freeze chops individually with sauce in plastic freezer bags or in containers. Reheat in a 350°F oven in a baking dish or roasting pan tightly covered with aluminum foil for about 25 minutes, until heated through.

FIESTA SAUSAGE

SERVES 4

When I cook this, I use turkey kielbasa; you can use pork, beef, or turkey as you wish. You may find a pair of tongs is easiest for handling the kielbasa slices.

2 Tbsp. vegetable oil
1 lb. Italian sausage, cut into ½-inch chunks
4 cloves garlic, chopped
2 medium onions, chopped
½ cup red wine
1 can (15 oz.) ready-to-eat Cuban-style
   black beans

1 cup canned diced tomatoes, with juice
¼ cup chopped fresh dill
1 tsp. dried sage
1 large yellow bell pepper, diced
1 cup frozen green beans
Salt, to taste
Freshly ground pepper, to taste

Heat oil in a large skillet and brown sausage on both sides. Remove and set aside. Add garlic and onions to pan and cook just until wilted. Drain fat from pan and add wine. Add sausage and all remaining ingredients. Lower heat, cover, and simmer for 20 minutes.

Freeze in containers or plastic freezer bags. To reheat on the stovetop or in the microwave, see page 6.

SAUSAGE, BEAN & APPLE CASSEROLE

SERVES 3

This is a sweet and comforting casserole: you'll love it!

1 Tbsp. vegetable oil
1 lb. pork sausage, sliced
1 can (30 oz.) kidney beans, rinsed and drained
1 large baking apple, peeled, cored and sliced
⅓ cup brown sugar

1 large onion, sliced
½ cup sliced celery
½ cup diced tomatoes with juice
Salt, to taste
Freshly ground pepper, to taste

Heat oven to 350°F. In a medium skillet over medium heat, heat oil and cook sausage, until lightly browned. Drain sausage of fat and transfer to a 9 x 13-inch baking pan. Add remaining ingredients and mix well.

Cover baking pan with aluminum foil and bake for 45 minutes. Remove cover and bake for an additional 15 minutes.

Freeze in plastic freezer bags. To reheat on the stovetop or in the microwave, see page 6. If reheating in the oven, be sure to cover container tightly.

LAMB ALLEGRA

SERVES 3 TO 4

1 can (16 oz.) tomato sauce
½ cup red wine
1 Tbsp. Worcestershire sauce
1 lb. ground lamb
1 onion, chopped
3 cloves garlic, chopped
1 cup cooked rice
Salt, to taste
Freshly ground pepper, to taste
1 tsp. dried basil

1 tsp. dried oregano
1 tsp. dried rosemary
¼ cup chopped fresh dill
¼ cup freshly grated ginger
½ cup sliced, pitted kalamata olives
1 small eggplant, peeled, thinly sliced
  and slices quartered
½ cup plain yogurt
1 cup crumbled feta cheese

Heat oven to 350°F. In a bowl, combine tomato sauce, wine and Worcestershire sauce.

Place lamb, onion, garlic, rice, seasonings, and olives in a 9-x-13-inch baking pan. Add ½ of the tomato sauce mixture and knead together thoroughly with your hands. Press ½ of the meat mixture evenly into pan. Layer eggplant evenly over meat. Press remaining meat mixture over eggplant.

Add yogurt and feta cheese to remaining tomato sauce mixture, stirring to combine. Spread over meat mixture. Bake for 1 hour. Cut into servings with a pancake turner.

Freeze each portion wrapped in aluminum foil. Reheat in a 350°F oven in same foil on a baking sheet for about 40 minutes.

KIELBASA WITH ARTICHOKES & GARBANZOS
SERVES 4

I use turkey kielbasa when I cook this, but it works well with pork, beef or other cooked varieties of sausage.

4 Tbsp. vegetable oil, divided
1 lb. smoked sausage, cut into ½-inch slices
4 cloves garlic, chopped
½ lb. mushrooms, sliced
½ cup dry white wine
1 can (14 oz.) artichoke hearts, drained and quartered

½ tsp. dried sage
½ tsp. dried thyme
½ tsp. dried rosemary
½ tsp. cayenne pepper
1 Tbsp. caraway seeds
1 cup canned garbanzo beans, rinsed and drained
½ cup chicken broth

Heat 2 tablespoons oil in a large skillet over medium heat. Add sliced sausage and brown on both sides, transferring to a plate as they brown. Add garlic and cook just until wilted, about 1 or 2 minutes. Set aside sausage and garlic. To same skillet, add mushrooms and sauté until lightly browned.

Drain fat from pan and add wine. Reduce heat, bring wine to a simmer, and return sausage and garlic to pan. Add all remaining ingredients. Simmer for 10 minutes.

Freeze in containers or plastic freezer bags. To reheat on the stovetop or in the microwave, see page 6.

MISSISSIPPI RED BEANS & RICE WITH SAUSAGE

SERVES 6

Did you know if you rinse and drain canned beans before using them, you remove a lot of the gas-causing properties? Rinsed beans also absorb more of the other flavors in your recipe.

2 Tbsp. olive oil
3 medium onions, peeled and thinly sliced
4 cloves garlic, minced
1 large green bell pepper, cut into small dice
1 lb. kielbasa or other cooked sausage, cut
   into ½-inch pieces
3 cans (15 oz. each) kidney beans, rinsed
   and drained

2 cups red wine
1 bay leaf
3 Tbsp. tomato paste
Salt, to taste
Freshly ground pepper, to taste
Tabasco Sauce, to taste
1 tsp. Worcestershire sauce
4–5 cups cooked white rice

Heat oil in a large skillet over medium heat. Sauté onions, garlic, and bell pepper until wilted. Add sausage slices and brown.

Add beans, wine, bay leaf, tomato paste, salt, pepper, Tabasco sauce and Worcestershire sauce. Reduce heat, cover and simmer for at least 1 hour, preferably 2 hours. Stir occasionally and add water if needed. Sauce should be reasonably thick. Remove bay leaf. Add rice and mix in.

Freeze in containers or plastic freezer bags. To reheat on the stovetop or in the microwave, see page 6.

KIELBASA MEAL-IN-A-POT

SERVES 4

Everyone will be back for seconds—guaranteed! Choose turkey, beef or pork kielbasa.

2 Tbsp. butter
1 medium onion, coarsely chopped
2 cups chicken or vegetable broth
½ cup water
1 lb. kielbasa, cut into ½-inch-thick slices
3 potatoes, thinly sliced

2 apples, peeled, cored, and cut into ½-inch dice
1 pkg. (8 oz.) coleslaw mix (shredded cabbage and carrots)
¼ tsp. cinnamon
½ tsp. dried thyme
½ tsp. dried savory

In a Dutch oven or other large pot, heat butter over medium heat and sauté onion until golden. Add broth and water. Add all other ingredients. Simmer, covered, for 45 minutes.

Freeze in containers. To reheat on the stovetop or in the microwave, see page 6. If reheating in the oven, be sure to cover container tightly.

MOROCCAN-STYLE LAMB STEW

SERVES 6

Middle-Eastern flavors and unusual ingredients enhance this lamb dish.
Serve with hot rice.

¼ cup olive oil

2½ lb. boneless lamb shoulder, cut into 1½-inch
    cubes

4 medium onions, quartered

2 Tbsp. finely chopped fresh ginger

2 cloves garlic, pressed

¼ cup chopped fresh parsley

Salt, to taste

Freshly ground pepper, to taste

¼ tsp. ground turmeric

1 can (14.5 oz.) diced tomatoes, with juice

1 cup raisins

⅔ cup almonds

2 hard-cooked eggs

In a Dutch oven or large pot with a tight-fitting lid, heat oil over medium heat. Cook lamb, turning to brown on all sides. Remove lamb from pot and set aside. Add onions, ginger, and garlic. Sauté, stirring, until onion is richly golden. Add parsley, salt, pepper, and turmeric and mix well. Return lamb to pot. Stir in tomatoes and juice. Bring to a boil, reduce heat, cover and simmer for 75 minutes, stirring occasionally.

While meat mixture is cooking, plump raisins: put them in a small bowl and cover with warm water. Toast almonds in a dry skillet over medium heat, tossing and turning to prevent burning, for about 4 minutes or until they become fragrant. Chop hard-cooked eggs. At end of cooking time, test meat for tenderness by piercing with a fork. When meat is done, turn off heat and mix in drained raisins, almonds, and eggs.

Freeze in plastic freezer bags. To reheat on the stovetop or in the microwave, see page 6.

BEEF & VEAL

OLD-FASHIONED POT ROAST

SERVES 4 TO 6

Ginger enhances the flavor of this pot roast. You don't need salt—there is enough in the soup. This goes well with noodles or potato pancakes.

2 lb. beef brisket

2 cans (10.5 oz. each) condensed onion soup, undiluted

1 cup water

½ cup red wine

⅓ cup tomato paste

¼ cup grated fresh ginger

2 tsp. paprika

6 cloves garlic, halved

Freshly ground pepper, to taste

2 bay leaves

½ tsp. dried oregano

Put all ingredients in a Dutch oven or large pot. Cover and simmer for at least 3 hours, until meat is tender. Check occasionally and add water if necessary. Remove bay leaves.

Slice meat before freezing with sauce in containers or freezer bags.

Reheat on the stovetop in a covered pot over medium-low to medium heat for 10 minutes, or longer depending on number of servings.

BEEF GOULASH BRATISLAVA-STYLE
SERVES 6

Serve this with noodles, garlic bread or another starch to soak up the rich gravy.

3 Tbsp. vegetable oil, divided
2 slices bacon, finely diced
2 large onions, chopped
1 green bell pepper, diced
1 medium tomato, chopped
3 cloves garlic, diced
1½ Tbsp. paprika

1 tsp. caraway seeds
Salt, to taste
Freshly ground pepper, to taste
2½ cups water, divided
2 lb. beef, cut into bite-size cubes
2 Tbsp. flour

In a large skillet over medium heat, heat 1 tablespoon of the oil. Add bacon, stirring, and cook until lightly browned. Add onion, bell pepper, tomato, and garlic and sauté for 2 minutes. Transfer to a Dutch oven or other large pot. Add paprika, caraway seeds, salt and pepper. Mix thoroughly. Add ½ cup of water, bring to a boil and reduce to a simmer.

In same skillet, heat remaining 2 tablespoons oil over medium heat. Add beef, browning lightly on all sides. As beef cubes brown, transfer to Dutch oven. Make sure there is at least ½-inch of liquid in pot and that it is simmering; stir and cover.

Cook for about 1½ hours. Check liquid level occasionally during cooking process and add water if needed. When meat is tender, add flour, stir until smooth and add remaining 2 cups water. Cook for 2 to 3 minutes, until gravy thickens.

Freeze in plastic freezer bags. To reheat on the stovetop or in the microwave, see page 6.

MEDITERRANEAN STEW

SERVES 4 TO 6

This stew requires planning ahead—the meat needs to marinate for at least 24 hours.

1½ cups red wine, prefer hearty Burgundy
  or Merlot

4 cloves garlic, thinly sliced

1 tsp. dried basil

Salt, to taste

Red pepper flakes, to taste

2 lb. beef, cut into ½-inch cubes

3 carrots, cut into thin slices

1 large onion, chopped

1 lb. mushrooms, sliced

6 plum tomatoes, or 4 regular tomatoes,
  coarsely chopped

1 cup pitted kalamata olives

1 tsp. dried oregano

1 tsp. dried basil

1 tsp. dried thyme

½ tsp. dried savory

2 bay leaves

1 cup vegetable or beef broth

In a bowl, mix together wine, garlic, basil, salt, and pepper flakes. Add meat, making sure it is well covered with marinade. Cover bowl. Refrigerate for 24 hours to 3 days.

Put meat and marinade into the bottom of a Dutch oven or similar large pot. Add all remaining ingredients. Cook over medium heat until mixture starts to boil. Reduce heat, cover and simmer for about 3 hours, or until meat is so tender that you can separate it with a fork. Check liquid level several times during cooking process, and add more broth, water or wine if needed. Remove bay leaves.

Freeze in plastic freezer bags. To reheat on the stovetop or in the microwave, see page 6.

MEATBALLS SWEDISH STYLE

SERVES 6

Applesauce is an unusual ingredient in these meatballs. You can substitute ground pork or turkey for part of the beef in this recipe.

MEATBALLS
2 lb. ground beef
1 cup cooked rice
2 cups unsweetened applesauce
2 medium onions, grated
1½ tsp. salt
Freshly ground pepper, to taste

SAUCE
1 beef bouillon cube
1 Tbsp. hot water
1 cup tomato sauce
½ cup red wine
1 tsp. ground coriander
1 tsp. garlic powder
½ tsp. dried thyme
½ tsp. dried oregano
1 tsp. brown sugar

Heat oven to 350°F. Knead together all meatball ingredients. Form into medium-size meatballs and place in a roasting pan or baking pan large enough to hold in one layer, preferably not touching.

Dissolve bouillon cube in water, crushing with a spoon and stirring. Mix with remaining sauce ingredients. Pour sauce over meatballs. Bake for 1 hour.

Freeze in plastic freezer bags. To reheat on the stovetop or in the microwave, see page 6.

BEEF ROMANA PICANTE

SERVES 3

Though this is easy to cook, the result is hearty and flavorful, with just a little bit of "bite." Go ahead, bite back —you'll like it.

Salt

1 lb. beef, cut into bite-size cubes

2 cloves garlic, chopped

1 large onion, diced

¼ cup red wine

¼ cup chopped, pitted black olives

1 can (14.5 oz.) diced tomatoes

½ tsp. dried rosemary

½ tsp. dried thyme

1 can (4.5 oz.) chopped green chiles

Salt the bottom of a large, preferably nonstick skillet over medium heat. Add beef, stirring until browned. Add garlic and onion. Cook, stirring intermittently, until onion and garlic are wilted. Add wine and reduce heat until liquid is just simmering. Add remaining ingredients and simmer for about 7 minutes.

Freeze in containers or plastic freezer bags. To reheat on the stovetop or in the microwave, see page 6.

PARTY BEEF IN WINE SAUCE

SERVES 8

I first tasted this at a party years ago, and the hostess gave me the recipe. Your friends and family will enjoy it as mine do. Serve over hot noodles or herbed rice.

Flour, for dredging
Salt, as needed
Freshly ground black pepper, as needed
¼ cup olive oil
2 Tbsp. butter or margarine
2 large or 3 medium onions, minced
4 cloves garlic, pressed

3 lb. top round steak, cubed
1 beef bouillon cube dissolved in 1 cup water
2 cups dry red wine, prefer Merlot or Cabernet Sauvignon
¼ tsp. dried oregano
1 bay leaf

Place enough flour in a shallow bowl to coat meat. Mix in salt and pepper to taste. Heat olive oil and butter over medium heat in a large skillet. Sauté onions and garlic until transparent and transfer to a Dutch oven or large pot. Dredge meat in flour, then brown quickly in skillet and transfer to Dutch oven.

Add remaining ingredients to Dutch oven, cover tightly and simmer for about 2 hours, or until meat is tender. Check periodically and add water if sauce becomes too thick. Remove bay leaf.

Freeze in containers or in plastic freezer bags. To reheat on the stovetop or in the microwave, see page 6.

STUFFED PEPPERS

SERVES 4

Easy, hearty and appealing, and it pleases the average man, if you happen to be cooking for one. Improve it with fresh herbs, if you have them .

4 firm large red and yellow bell peppers,
    flat-bottomed
3 cans (8 oz. each) tomato sauce, divided
1 Tbsp. Worcestershire sauce
1½ tsp. dried basil
1½ tsp. dried oregano

Salt, to taste
Freshly ground pepper, to taste
4 cloves garlic, pressed, divided
1 lb. ground beef
¾ cup cooked rice
1 medium onion, chopped

Heat oven to 350°F. Slice tops from bell peppers and scoop out seeds and ribs. Reserve tops. Place upright in a large pot with enough water to cover and simmer until crisp-tender, about 8 minutes. Do not overcook. Place upright in a baking pan or a casserole just large enough to hold them.

In a bowl, mix together tomato sauce, Worcestershire sauce, basil, oregano, salt and pepper to taste and ¼ of the pressed garlic. Mix well.

In another bowl, mix together meat and rice. Add ¾ cup of the tomato sauce mixture, remaining garlic, and onion. Knead together until well mixed. Fill peppers with meat-rice mixture, mounding if necessary. Pour remaining tomato sauce mixture over and around stuffed peppers. Replace tops on peppers.

Bake, uncovered, for 50 to 55 minutes. Freeze in individual containers tall enough to hold peppers. To reheat on the stovetop or in the microwave, see page 6.

GINGER BEEF STRIPS WITH MUSHROOMS

SERVES 6

Here are more East and West flavors in a skillet stir-fry.

3 oz. dried imported mushrooms
2 Tbsp. peanut oil
2 lb. beef, cut into strips
8 cloves garlic, sliced

¼ cup grated fresh ginger
½ cup red wine
5 Tbsp. soy sauce
1 can (14 oz.) Chinese baby corn, drained

Reconstitute mushrooms for 1 hour in a bowl of warm water to cover. While mushrooms are soaking, heat oil in a large nonstick skillet over medium-high heat. Cook beef strips, stirring constantly, until no longer pink. Add garlic and ginger and cook until garlic is wilted. Add wine and soy sauce.

Squeeze mushrooms to remove excess liquid and reserve 1 cup. Add baby corn, mushrooms, and reserved liquid to skillet. Reduce heat and simmer for 5 minutes.

Freeze in containers. To reheat on the stovetop or in the microwave, see page 6.

PICADILLO À LA CATALANA

SERVES 4

This ground beef recipe is rich with Spanish flavors. Serve it with rice.

2 Tbsp. olive oil
1 small onion, finely chopped
1 lb. ground beef
Salt, to taste
Freshly ground pepper, to taste
Garlic powder, to taste

½ bottle (3.5 oz. bottle) capers with
  all liquid from bottle
½ cup raisins
½ cup canned diced tomatoes, drained,
  with ⅓ cup of the canned juice
¼ cup diced stuffed olives

In a large skillet, heat oil over medium heat and cook onion until soft but not brown. Add meat, breaking up and browning. Add all remaining ingredients, except olives, and cook for 10 minutes. Add olives.

Freeze in containers. Reheat on the stovetop for about 15 minutes; see page 6.

EASY BEEF GOULASH

SERVES 6 TO 8

This recipe easily becomes Beef Stroganoff: use sliced beef, reduce amount of tomato sauce, add some dill, and add a pint of sour cream after removing from heat. If you freeze Beef Stroganoff, add the sour cream after reheating process—not before freezing. Serve with hot noodles or garlic bread.

3 Tbsp. vegetable oil
4 medium onions, chopped
3 bell peppers, red and yellow, cut into strips
2 lb. mushrooms, sliced
2 lb. beef round steak, bite-size pieces
Salt, to taste
Freshly ground pepper, to taste
2 cans (about 10.25 oz. each) beef gravy

2 cans (about 10.25 oz. each) mushroom gravy
1 can (15 oz.) tomato sauce
Garlic powder, to taste
2 tsp. dried oregano
5 drops Tabasco Sauce, or to taste
2 Tbsp. Worcestershire sauce
½ cup red wine

Heat oil in a large skillet over medium heat. Sauté onions until lightly golden. Transfer to a Dutch oven or large pot. Put pepper strips in skillet, cook just until wilted. Transfer to Dutch oven. Sauté mushrooms until they begin to turn brown. Transfer to Dutch oven. Brown meat, seasoning with salt and pepper, to taste. Transfer to Dutch oven.

Add all remaining ingredients and simmer, covered, for about 1½ hours, until meat is tender and flavors have blended. Check gravy consistency periodically and add water if needed. If too thin, remove lid at end of cooking period to reduce.

Freeze in plastic freezer bags. To reheat on the stovetop or in the microwave, see page 6.

CHILI CON CARNE

SERVES 3

There is no one "right" way to cook chili. It's fun to vary the meat, the beans, and the other flavors.

2 Tbsp. vegetable oil
4 medium onions, coarsely chopped
1 lb. ground beef
1 can (14.5 oz.) diced tomatoes, with juice
1 can (15 oz.) black beans, or kidney beans, rinsed and drained

2 heaping Tbsp. chili powder, or to taste
½ tsp. dried oregano
½ tsp. garlic powder
Cayenne pepper to taste, optional
Salt, to taste
Freshly ground pepper, to taste

In a large skillet, heat oil over medium heat and sauté onions until golden. Add beef, breaking it up, and cook until beginning to brown. Add tomatoes with juice and beans.

Add remaining ingredients, reduce heat, cover and simmer for about 1 hour. Check periodically and add water if needed. Taste and adjust seasonings if needed. If chili is too soupy, remove lid and cook until liquid level is reduced.

Freeze in containers. To reheat on the stovetop or in the microwave, see page 6.

VEAL MARSALA

SERVES 4

This recipe can also be made with chicken or turkey cutlets. Either way, it is elegant enough to serve to guests.

Salt, to taste
Freshly ground pepper, to taste
Flour to dredge veal
1½ lb. veal cutlets or scallops, pounded
3 Tbsp. olive oil
½ lb. mushrooms

4 cloves garlic
2 cups chicken broth
1 cup Marsala wine or dry white wine
1½ Tbsp. lemon juice
1 pinch dried marjoram
½ tsp. dried thyme

Mix salt and pepper with enough flour to coat veal. Dredge veal in flour mixture. Heat oil in a large skillet over medium heat and sauté mushrooms until golden. While sautéing mushrooms, add garlic to wilt but not brown.

When mushrooms and garlic are ready, push them to the side and quickly brown veal on both sides.

When veal is browned, add broth, wine, lemon juice, and herbs to the pan. Blend and push garlic and mushrooms back into middle of pan. Reduce heat, cover and simmer for about 30 minutes.

Freeze in containers. To reheat on the stovetop or in the microwave, see page 6.

INDEX